LANDSCAPE WITH BLOODFEUD

LANDSCAPE WITH BLOODFEUD

WENDY BARNES

UNIVERSITY OF MASSACHUSETTS PRESS

Amherst and Boston

ISBN 978-1-62534-641-4 (paper)

Designed by Deste Roosa

Set in Adelle and Adobe Caslon Pro

Printed and bound by Books International, Inc.

Cover design by Sally Nichols

Cover photo: *Peeling Wall Paper,* © View7 | Dreamstime.com

Library of Congress Cataloging-in-Publication Data

Names: Barnes, Wendy, author.

Title: Landscape with bloodfeud / Wendy Barnes.

Description: Amherst : University of Massachusetts Press, [2022] | Series:
   Juniper prize for poetry

Identifiers: LCCN 2021054472 (print) | LCCN 2021054473 (ebook) | ISBN
   9781625346414 (paperback) | ISBN 9781613769171 (ebook) | ISBN
   9781613769188 (ebook)

Subjects: LCGFT: Poetry.

Classification: LCC PS3602.A775656 L36 2022 (print) | LCC PS3602.A775656
   (ebook) | DDC 811/.6—dc23/eng/20211108

LC record available at https://lccn.loc.gov/2021054472

LC ebook record available at https://lccn.loc.gov/2021054473

British Library Cataloguing-in-Publication Data

A catalog record for this book is available from the British Library.

—Where do you folks live at?
—Between the A and the T.

C. D. Wright

A sea of griefs is not a proscenium,
and a man who wails is not a dancing bear.

Aimé Césaire

CONTENTS

LANDSCAPE WITH BLOODFEUD

WITNESS, THE LEVEE

1

This is what I mean to save:

Braid of moss, fish hull, temper
of cloud. For years in the pre-storm
inertia, purple dawn, wrack wing.
Jackdaw and blackbird, static, a blue
copse. Barbed wire anchors
the asphalt city limits,
then cane fire, swamp gas,
tar, burning of. The old smoke drifts
backward and inward, blood
orange, persimmon. Oil boom
hangover tunes leak from morning
bars. Beer and trumpets,
their hollow cheer. What I can save
is crumbled brick and cinder
block, forehead ash. Palms
rustle, bless the white-smocked
children drifting across the still city
square. You are so used to concrete
sky, hush afternoon, flash
of future casts your profiles
in lightning. Faces tip
upward and open
to rain. Mosquito, butterfly,
Luna moth whipped brittle landward
on tightening wind; late sky,
birds drop from.

2

This is what I have to give:

Every season falls through you
at once, wind-crush, wind and ghost
migrations climb through a hole
in the century, lurch over land
and sea. The old injuries—
voices in drywall, cedar post, sidewalk,
all sunk. Vacuum of breath,
concrete hush of backache, lashwhip,
history. You swallow all the silt
that ever rained down a river.
You know what waits
in the gulf, the way it grips the throat,
chokes like heat, the way it can cripple
like legend—gothic fangs sink the ships,
voodoo claws pop the rafts.
What waits out in the gulf,
an animal fear that swells,
then gallops inland, rafter high,
to erase what you once knew
of your own secrets. Still,
you wind yourselves in sheets
of rain that reach from past to past,
then loose you, drifting, like late terns
untethered from a liquid core.
Firecracker, gunshot, tapshoe.
You are so used to eating storm.
You turn your backs, but I can see
what courses toward us.
It is colorless, sure of hoof.

I

THE REVENANT QUARRELS WITH WEATHER

I kicked loose from those local
squalls, blew north, looked down years

later from a different state, one free
of crepe myrtle, mustard greens,

grits, the telescope reflecting
my one big eye.

What breed of citizen refuses
warmth, disputes a river's swerves

into myth, decries bees,
their tangled flight lines? Who casts

her bone dice across nostalgia's
ruined map? Once the alligator jaws

find me again, drop me back
into the archive of storm, I fall

through its flat, migraine
light, run my hand down pages

squirming with memory,
chant their script in a bad

accent, riff a borrowed
creole back into blank mouths.

At the museum of our civic
remains, in its animal damp, I remember

a little, return to the crucial
ligaments, what tore, I wander

out, name the vacancies, number
the rubble. Garden, river, or trouble,

everything grows beyond
daub walls, earth walls, concrete.

I want to take it all back.
That's like holding the tide, says the tide.

You think you can undo thunder?
says thunder.

I chant these spells
against weather,

but I am not as fluent as rain
or the wind that pronounces the waves.

REFLECTION IN MUDDY WATER

Black cypress sketched
in first light,
longing taps its snare drum.

A whooping crane untucks
her face from her wing,
bugles the day's first notes

over the water's
quiet coaxing.

Among the reeds,
a rabbit shakes off
sleep's gray caul.

And there it is again, my drama
of description, drawn out
beyond what's chaste.

Why do I see my own face
stare back at me, even
from this fluid state of sold matter:

red mud sluices down the bank,
drooping like my flesh.

But this coupling, too, is false.
My mind is just a thicket of myself
trapping everything it finds.

I resolve to be more modest,
wonder how. I resolve to be
more like a pine wood—

no, an orchard—
natural in its art but ordered.
I cup the seeds in my hand,

but they scatter
like lovers, each sprung sapling his own
stubborn column of light.

So much for love
and modesty.

Why can't I stop romancing
the landscape? I grasp at it,

claim it for mine.
I guess I'm dead-set
on rejection.

A landscape never loves you back
or shows you who you are.

It never feels despair.
I am the one who crumbles
in the middle

like a hillful of ants
crushed beneath a boot,
who lingers in the dirt

till I molder,
blowflies hatching
from my fingertips.

Now I *am* this landscape.
I'm the bog, the swamp
the *marais*—my new name:

Big Muddy Maw.
My nether aching
never was for love.

I won't be tamed,
no kitchen garden
waiting to oblige with knife-deep,

even furrows.
Then why do I still cave
and settle?

I must be sinking.
I guess I'll sing my own lament.

HOW BIENVILLE ENLIGHTENS
THE BOTTOMLAND, 1718

What crude god fashioned such a river,
its lunatic meanders, trees convulsed
with chirps and screams, their green so green
it blackens, lures the sunlight in to die.
The bank surrenders beneath my sword.
I claim this higher ground to raise the future
convent, the customs house—cathedral
to our enterprise—leave the marshlands for tents
and lean-tos, make them bulwarks against storm.
I'll refute wilderness with a grid, align
the plan for an ideal city upon this square
league of land. I march the regiment through bramble
and mire, startling hoary pines, giant moths
to heavy flutter, march into a hut village,

into a stillness. A lone mockingbird trumpets
the royal anthem. All other species elude us.
Some stare wide-eyed from shadows, from beyond
our taxonomy. I refute yellow fever,
flood, I refute heat, the stench of rot
that rises from my men. They cop their hilts, randy
for a fight. I know the depth of their gouge-
longing. Mules thrum in harness, rebuke
seethes in the river's rising, rebuke
of warsong stains the night, a shriek that pierces,
somehow known to me, like an echo
still sounding forth since the world's punishing
birth. I blast the cannon's clean rejoinder,
order a fusillade from the muskets.

Through dove-colored fog, I force all natural forms—
the animal, the element, the very sea—
                              to yield.

AFFLICTION PARISH

The plant puffs a final cloud through nuclear
smokestacks. Under the numb of sunrise, our synapses

atrophied in sweet tea, we watch the floodwaters
surge then retreat and spit out our doublewides,

sprawled belly-up and helpless. The river's no better,
it branches out, spins its slow arms loose

and tempts the Gulf to come on in and swamp
the turbines. Hey there, gale force and heavy drizzle.

Between dinner and supper, we watch cotton balls
rot in their bolls. The pressure drops, some baby squalls

wash away everybody's duck blinds
and righteous rage. We toss our empties

in parking lot weeds, find the drunken union rep
heel-drug and drowned in his optimism. Past the courthouse,

the sad single oil well churns its mud-butter.
Welcome, recovery task force, and whoops,

looks like you mistook our unemployment line
for a load-bearing wall, but why not? You need to rest

the new foundation on somebody's bones, plus,
our sorry nuclei are always wrong.

The church shuts up early on payday, but we go in
for bootleg faith and any remedy that peels us

for a minute from our wet skins and thunder counting.
Hello, trespass and B and E, pecans batter the squad car,

little fists of grief the trees shake down.
The prison gate clangs against its hinges,

somebody's muffler chugs
Told you so, told you so, telling us so.

CITYSCAPE WITH CARNIVAL

Bonesmen at sunrise, Indian calls and lip sweat,
bless our pickled hearts, the river's alligator
ripples. Night Train, Sazerac, Wild
Irish. Irish Channel, horses pull the ferry
through the lock. Let's secondline
up Basin Street, follow Wild
Magnolia, shout under backbeat drum.

Riverboat, redfish, catfish, turtle
soup. St. Claude for po-boy, b-boy, t-boy, dirty white
rice. Fireworks stipple Rampart, gunshot,
cops. Let's zydeco across the quarter
to the cathedral. Damp t-shirts, ball gowns,
top hats, g-strings, pray us up, holy a/c. Pass the J
across the pew. Hallelujah, fireheart, fresh baked.

Riverscape, mudmouth, bonesmen at dusk.
Pale indigo fog. Pass the plastic cups,
follow the horses. *Flambeaux* riders
light the levee bonfires, heartshine.
Have mercy, Mississippi, old mudheart churns its redbean
blood through spillway, bayou, veins that bend
the water's tonic note down to the Gulf.

PHOTOGRAPH FROM ANGOLA
PENITENTIARY, 1935

There is a hole in the fabric
of the grass.

The iron sweatbox
hunkers on its haunches,

squatting, a coffin-shaped canker
in the would-be pastoral

scene, its dead metal alive
with buzzing. It vibrates

on the screen,
set to burst its rigid outline,

the frame
that anchors its meaning.

It hums with the muffled voices
of its formerly entombed,

lifesparks smothered
inside that airless place,

inside a spite
so thick, you couldn't see

your own hand.
A man forgot

the road he walked
to get here, the one

that led him to the end
of mercy.

And I have found
this crypt

among the cheerless public
archive, black-and-white photos

of cells, uniforms, eyes,
the remains of all those lost.

By what right
do I click its image, enlarge,

will its lid to open
just so I can look inside?

LANDSCAPE WITH ACCENT

We don't have any vistas
to pull your eye beyond the tree line,
just a view of Black Bayou

topping its banks. But jump
in the truck. I brought some baitworms,
a cooler full of Jax. Welcome

to the parish of fenced-in
vernacular, where the land hunkers low
like a toad,

to the "sportsman's paradise,"
where you can kiss a catfish or a cross
for luck, to beat back disaster.

We'll gut the catch at the house,
but look out. That neighbor's dog
will take your finger off

if you wander past the fence,
past your own clipped consonants.
We'll crack another tall boy,

watch the pelicans
and overtime paychecks
flap away, dissolve in puffs of mist.

The workweek kicks shut
like a Red Wing to the eye.
Get in, let's drive thru

the daiquiri take-out,
where the cashier flicks
her cigarette at us, and drive around

until the road begins to bounce.
Somebody busted the porch light.
We trip through the glow that oozes

between the truck door and the porch,
wallow in the blackout between Friday
and our resurrection, pressed then dropped

into our Sunday selves. But in the parish
of our unquenchable dirt,
there is no bottom,

there is no communion,
just the slow vowel's soft
center we keep chewing.

The dawn smiles, missing a canine,
incisors shot through with aluminum.
A hangover pulls its endless red bandanna

through our skulls. Could we ever break free
from the parish of screaming Yazoo
mowers? Get your tool belt.

Let's take the river road,
where Monday morning fog concertinas
the top of the levee. Listen,

can you hear that marshland
raising hell as the water gulps
another of its soggy acres?

I'd rather drown than surrender
our warm, drawling soil.
Down at the jobsite,

laughing gulls screech overhead,
The concrete mixer rumbles,
dumps its gray certainty

into the hole.
It knows that dirt belongs to no one.
I mount the Caterpillar backhoe,

work the stick controls,
smooth and soothe the tangles
of black earth, religiously.

THE HUNT

Rubber boots huddled
by the truck, a passed flask.
Lit cigarettes,

headlamps like nebulae.
Their lightbeams swung drunken arcs
that slashed the pine trunks.

When I was nine
I thought I was a clean
and certain thing,
like the snap of a bone.

I slipped my knife from its sheath,
tested the blade
on the tip of my thumb,

set Belle loose
from her lead. She scattered
a curse of night thrush
from the scrub.

We descended into the swamp,
its bowl of sound—night peeper,
bullfrog, cicada—
a rising crescendo.
Belle howled after the scent.

My dad followed with the rifle.
I watched the machete
swing from his belt loop.

Then forepaws planted
on the pine trunk,
and up above,

the silver aria
of her eyes. Her whiskers.
Her delicate fingers

clutched and unclutched
the branch as if to still its shifting
beneath her fear.

Before the shot, I thought
a bullet pierced a body clean,
the tiny corpse folding neatly
into its fall
like a handkerchief.

Before that shot,
I thought I was a certain
kind of animal,

but when it hit,
I hissed and chittered. I howled
louder than any grown man.

Then I fell and am
still falling, sinking under
the velvet stain,

am the raccoon tumbling forever
into the jaws of the bloodhound,
am the bloodhound
bellowing up
at the moonless sky.

II

LANDSCAPE WITH BLOODFEUD

1

I am not a hemi half-ton
pickup, toolbox in the back, gunrack
and deer-painted cab,

but I learned to drive one
down a shell road,
spewing dust and leaded fumes.

I am not a Remington
30 ought 6
with bolt action, standoff
choke and soft point
cartridges,

but I learned how to shoot it, align
the iron sights, center
the innocent object, squeeze, explode
the difference between it
and me.

Nor am I a used
14 x 80 singlewide
mobile home—

we bought it from a Florida woman
with wrists covered in suicide scars,
dragged it around from town to town,

truck tires burning up I-10
across the Panhandle,
back to Louisiana.

Our own home.
But home is
the permanent question,
the always unsteady
premise.

In this version,
my dad is a pair of Carhartt overalls
filled with bulletholes
and a pinch of snuff,

my mother a bundle
of wattles and wails,
spit and snakebites that vie
for her breath.

We find some land and
wrestle it down,
hack a homestead
out of scrub brush

and a fallen barn,
plant the trailer,
some tomatoes and corn,

move in and let
the formaldehyde
begin to pit our lungs.

In this version,
I am matted hair and terrycloth
tubetop, a film
of grime around its mouth.

My brother—cutoffs, wad
of bubblegum,
and holey rubber boots.

He hands me a cream soda
and we try to rake the yard rubble
into some kind of
sense, tend our family
sharecrop.

My rake gets caught in weeds, his
grabs loamy dirt that sticks
between the tines,

so we get down and dig
with our hands
scooping up mouthfuls,

spider mites and roly-polies
popping
between our teeth.

2

I never wanted to be
any specific place
on the page,
or in a definite personal
location,

rooted trailer-like, tied down
with metal straps and bolted
to the earth.

To have a home.
But home is still
the empty set, the ever-shifting
proposition.

And now I'm grown,
I roam the earth
trailerless.

Everywhere I go I look
for their eyes, the beasts
of my same salt, same dirty grease.

They may not look like me.
If they see me on the bus,
they may not recognize my face, but they
will know me by my beer breath
and familiar rage.

The kind that still carries my brother
on its waves, their crests
breaking into barfights,

the kind that eats me
from the inside
like the pesticides
that bled into our well.

And everywhere I go I cross
the same scrubby farmland,
crooked bridge,
same black water.

But one of me will always be back
in that 1980s living room,
hand on the joystick,
she is made of French fry grease
and Atari asteroid dust, she is

American, a hunk
of mismatched parts
Frankencultured, zombiefaced,
empty empty on the inside

but for the thumping bass
that fills my brother's tricked-out
Chevy Nova when we cruise to school.

One of me permanently hunkers
in a squatty desk
reading that hardback history textbook

with peach-faced cartoon people
engaged in guiltless
murder and light manufacture.

That's where I could first feel history
inside me, pulsing.
I may not know my ancestors,

but I carry their atrocities, I carry
my Britishness like a plague-
colored taint in my personal codex,

on the vellum, blacking a hole
through the vellum, likewise my Spaniard,
and German, and other suchlike,
wayback kin.

I carry their violence. They are spoiling
for a fight inside my cells,
my landed gentry, admirals, explorers
slipping off their waistcoats,
flexing their biceps,

my thieves and peasants, shoeless soldiers
whipping off their shirts,
bowing up their chests.

These are my bloods that battle
across barbed wire and trenches,
over mountain holler and moor, bloodfeuds
that bruise and purple on.

Inside my guts
boil the Boer Wars,
Tippecanoe, Antietam,
and the Easter Rising,

some pilgrims,
and a paste of poor and chewed-up
white people digested forever
into ghosty mud.

But I can't reconcile
the record:
An ancestor worked to death
as an indentured servant,

another a bigamist dirt farmer
still rich enough to enslave
a person
whose only known legacy
is his one name,
Cephus.

I know I am nothing
to the anguished center
of this story, yet I can't help
speaking it in circles around myself.

As in—who is there to answer
for these deeds, my deeds,
or not my deeds?
Ancestral guilt breathes poison

through its long sleep,
poison that seeps
from my own pores like a swarm.

Yes, this is my scourge
of flies, and there are fangs
inside me like devil buds,
these fangs in the gut.

I cut them out.
They sprout back
every spring.

But surely I exaggerate this shame
just to give myself a pass—
do I think I'm virtuous because I claim
these past crimes?

3

One of me is back on the homestead
sounding out some pointless apologies,
but this is no place for dwelling
on the bygone or wondering aloud.

The bloodhound has bolted from the pen,
and there is a permanent brushfire
to the east that is always
burning this way.

My grandfather rolls up
in his pickup,
hangs his cigarette out the window,

waves me over
tells me, *Grab your machete*
and hack out your place

and keep hacking
until you reach the beating pith,
and hack that too—and then what?

And then I am here in the middle
of this dead landscape
with a flimsy voice for company
since I've killed everything.

Every landscape
is a long howl in the night
that someone's broken with
machetes or garrotes

or casual dreaming. We have said,
Hey, come here and grabbed that howl
by the throat.

Then we built invisible fences.
They make a close-
fitting cell that moves when we do

from parish to parish.
It throbs with heat,
each inmate guards
her own perimeters.

My brother has plans
for the Apocalypse.
When a siren sounds
or we hear shrieking in the woods,

we grab the guns,
we defend the trailer
like Huns, no, Romans,
no, Thundercats,

my brother's got
the ammo belt. We are unholstered,
safeties off, in the pee-smelling
tomato patch.

We listen for enemies
but hear only rain
ticking on the trailer roof.

It's then I know
we have learned nothing.

I am in the garden muffled
under a misery of ghosts
who want to hold me or to choke me.

One ghost slips into my arms,
but I don't know
how to console it,
so I crush it,
out of love.

III

THE REVENANT RETRACES HER STEPS

How perilous is it to choose
not to love the life we're shown?

Seamus Heaney

When I got the chigger under chigger itch, when I forded

the river, found the same cows on the other side, it was time.

When my people of heavy stock turned their hammers

to the sky, hacked out great blue chunks,

and then the ghosts of those old conquerors

oozed back up through my veins. It was time

when I'd wagered away my fortune in earthworms,

when the radio played only staticky news, and confusion

ran so deep I had to look up for the low down.

It was time when I almost caught the beat but lost it

down a sinkhole, when my brass band marchers fell out

under the sun, and rogue parades danced down my alley

all day every day. When the fish kill, the schooled-up trout smells

lost their magic. It was time when I could no longer taste

a coming storm's ozone on the wind, and I could hold only two cupfuls

of brown water at once, night damp went terminal, crawfish keeled over,

unhinging their pincers, then friends forgot my name,

qualm's catfish barb stuck in my throat, the last mosquito

of my hope was diagnosed. I held out my palm and caught

a single drop of rain, and it was then

I looked down the open road.

SELF-PORTRAIT AS SOLID, LIQUID, GAS

Flood rolls through me, sheds
its oyster shells and silt. I remain

a crossroads in a floodplain stuttering
with repetition—bottlecaps and hunchbacked

stalks slumped row upon row, silent as my stunted
convictions. I want the fluency of finches' wings

but am ponderous lips, split plum and muscadine,
flesh dropped from the vine, the leaf so tired

it rots and, rotted, yellows to black—as parking lot
asphalt: illegible. I lie down in that word and dissolve

into a field of muddled desires packed so thick
no fate can enter. The pitfires

burn the sugarcane, acid and sweet,
boil away the useless juice. I should be that sticky

ethane fume. I once sifted
the petroleum-scented loam of my future

in my own hands, planted pockets of hope
in a lonely girlhood's flat expanse, faith in my downy

rebirth, in rock and mineral, wood and animal.
A sickly pine inched up, unspooled its needles,

cast its puny authority over the field mice,
over the feed troughs and the weeping.

Steel blades bore the meat from cypress trunks; drill heads
press seeds into the dirt, plant new sorghum late and low, the runoff

spills its syrup cold into another state. If only I could
drift skyward, where the fearless rise like heat.

Their voices coast on rippled space,
and gravitational waves

rehearse their scales in a vacuum of light.
I could be paraphrased there, from my atoms,

as a pinprick point of sun
in that refrigerated blank,

I could escape all three,
water, air, and me.

SOUTH OF THE NARCISSUS

Am I to dangle here forever, strangled
in vines of kudzu and sloth, or at least until

the yellow dawn, love's catalytic converter of lies?
Each vault of the tire swing brings me elsewheres

too bright to touch, a cloud deletes the moon. Forswearing
the charms of gardenia, magnolia—all the achy blossoms

of Ascension Parish, lit from inside with chemical nutrients—
I wait and wait in the dark for the cruisy boy in his daddy's Cadillac

to come leaking oil down the driveway, where last weekend
I was nearly deleted in his backseat, damn it, me

and stolen tequila, a tang like fertilizer steaming up
the windows. I know there is a world, I have seen it

online, but past the cypress trees, Bayou Narcisse exhales puffs
of methane, reminds me of my mosquito life and how alone

I carve these puzzles in mud. Tell me why all-night-
refinery lights burn like tinfoil fairies in pony hair.

They say they flood the dark for planes and shiftwork,
but I know a sweet thing who simpers her way

to the top of the tower, hugs her crush tight
through a tattered nightdress. The girl gazes out over the swamp,

thinks that beau will spell her escape, but the boy
forgets her face, spells her name S-L-U-T whore.

I swing on into the dawn and want that creeping sun
to tell me and tell me straight

what I already know. The liquors of industry ooze
downward. Poor girls, we're tumbled and drowned

in those runnels before we ever get our elsewheres,
little dollbones loosed from our sockets.

INTERIOR WITH LOCKED DOORS

I stand accused of brash and bluster
on the netherest tip of the deadest star.
    I pace this ward alone.

You've never known my like,
    I am weathervane, tuning fork,
measure of men and rain, whatever

    gauges against me,
I win. Or I did.
But then they caught me

and my bombast halfway
to Shreveport, the squarecut crewjaws,
    called in to manhandle

all of us broken-
    necked flowers. They spit snuff juice
at my feet,

drugged me and dragged me
to lockup.
    I tripped and fell

into a pantomime
of apology, shadowboxing
    with my shame.

    Nethermost, silenced person,
I thought I was nobody's
mouth harp, pastie tassel, fistful

of hair. I'd built my makeshift self
    a swashbuckling thing,
forged a shield of cardboard,

    I was Ajax, I was Thor,
shedding flame from the booney
hills across the wide-eyed

plain, reeling through the whole rude
continent, then run down
        in a cul-de-sac and mouthing

sorries I didn't mean.
        But I meant it when I left
their drive-in, their five and dime,

        their souped-up cruisers
smashed in the Phillips station
parking lot, left the stars permanently
        fractured

by those cracks in their windshields.
Now I'm caught I can't stop
        asking me the wrong questions,

        all my papier-mâché
dogs gone meek, only muzzled
squealing from my subterranean
        pains.

And did I turn wrong.
        The searchlights ache,
a cellful of spites

bears down and bleeds me.
        I do not turn wrong.
        Or want wrong,

not the loosening wind on my face,
not even my name
traced in dust. Just some brute
        morning light.

        And listen,
my voice,
my voice throws new shoots
        out into it.

THE COLLABORATOR

Complicity smells like blood, like squirrel meat
at suppertime. Gristle, tendon in your teeth,
sit at the table, you've got to eat
what's in your bowl, raw fish, crawfish fat, shrimp
with eyes and veins. You have to eat this
little dove fried whole, crunch the twiggy bones.
Wild aftertaste runs on like rats fleeing
from the barn. They scream as yard dogs
tear them from their holes and shake, then the clubs,
shovels, pitchforks. Rodents, so many,
your throat tastes blood in the air, even
from the screenporch. Get in the boat and bait
your hook. Worm juice soaks your whitebread.
You will always taste that too. Self-loathing

feels like a bite of the young cow you've loved
from a calf—swatting flies from her face—
nubby teeth nibble your baby-fat palms. Now,
chew your calf. You can be made to swallow chunks
of her, even with your throat clenched—don't you
run away. Split open these live bivalves,
splay them gasping on beds of ice. When
deer die by gunshot, arrow, when a deer
dies by your brother's hand, help him string
the torso between two trees. Her head lies there
girl-faced in profile. You can almost taste
the last grassy morning of her life.
Watch wordless as he pulls her skin from her
flesh, a teenaged mammal, now take the knife.

HOW MY FOREBEARS WHITEWASH HISTORY

The story goes I come from a rigid line
of swamp-carving brogues and pogues.
We fanned forth, cut a saw palmetto

path from alluvial berth in Virginia's Great Dismal
to points south spanned by water oak
and superstition, slashed through the Carolinas

to Okefenokee and westward, by donkey
or wagon, rust-mauled three-
or four-on-the-floor. Never ones

to want it easy, any rotten condition, gangrene
state, or bog pit would do us fine. "Pioneer folk,"
the kind who'd herd up against a stranger and cow

all the other underdogs. We'd stake
a home in porous ground—convicts, pickers,
fisherfolk, sap tappers. Never asked

for hope. We preferred to loot or lick the bottoms
of 'shine stills, sumps, and hollers,
swinging our fiddles and banjos, plucky

as you please. Generations of us punched
a living from bottomland and quarrelsome
beasts. But the story runs cold,

                runs into blanks and dead-end
dirt crossings and rusted railroad tracks
that run up on our old barn

and on my grandfather.
I find him outside banging on a crank case.
        Sure, we wore the sheets, he allows,

but he swears we never broke a single
        person's body. *It was a social club,* he says,
We mostly just went to get drunk.

A loon wails from inside
the marsh.

I turn and look for some shape to the absence
        the lie leaves behind,

but I can see only a hole
out in the piney, out in the suffering
woods.

THE PROFITEERS
THE CHICAGO, ST. LOUIS, AND NEW ORLEANS RAILROAD, 1878

Every way they look, the North Star quivers.
Why not forge our own welcome, descend
with horse teams and steel ambition, rescale
their maps, build them up from the ashes
of their scorns and scorched crops. Those inert
acres pine for speed; dead dirt begs the harrow.
We'll have 'em haul and hew, use whoever brings
their broke-handed backwork—clay eaters,
chawbacons, freedmen struck dumb with their luck,
feed 'em on hardtack and trust. Sweat sets weary
bodies in our orbit, hunger yokes them in place.
We'll crosshatch their future with tracks, tunnel
new frontiers through the lusty interior, trailing
all the little orphans and their beggar bowls.

THE CADILLAC CLUB, 1922

Fancy said besides
      the deckhand, the lineman,
  and the roustabout,
    he was the only one.

He played her bass, and when she sang,
she ran that room, she cheapened
    herself with swigs
      of Kentucky Gold,

ragamuffin of jagged melodies,
baloney, and homemade glad rags.

Drink it, she sang, the half-light
was sweating the trio's shrill honey.

She gave them her ragtime colors and gin,
    the drum's hot peril,

and the suicide piano wire
her backbeat rhythm
    sprung free.

JITTERBUG, 1953

drank Schlitz or Dixie in the kitchen
in her curlers, slippers slapping her footbacks
    to Peggy Lee.

Storm wind slammed the screendoor,
and she remembered
that time she couldn't sleep,
    so she limped past the plant
    to the Texaco
with a nickel for a coke,

and there he was, bad faith on a stick
with a handsome head of hair,
    and that was it.
She liked to be a little scared.

    What's the rhubarb in there?
She yawped at the living room,
where kids dragged a grubby doll baby
by the hair and fingernails.

WETLANDS, WHEREIN THE ORPHANS

Walls moaned, sweated, a water moccasin
spooled 'round the table leg,
the console TV popped and sputtered.
Batten the mizenmast, you landhounds,
you stumblebums! The orphan house hovered
on its stilts; the matron chirped out orders: *Skitter*
up to the attic with you, turn the broadsail!
There was no mast, we never really
shipped, but we were ready—we kids,
the *gosses,* woke each day as brown water snaked
between the floorboards. We'd bail out the mess
and schoolroom, lower decks, then paddle
around outside in a five-gallon bucket or atop
the rusted hood of a '68 Plymouth.
And chères, the manic land redeems.
Provides. By noon it sucked its waters back,
the dandelions bloomed, leaving not a sip
of sludge, leaving dinner—a nutria carcass,
a squirrel, a possum big as a stew pot.
Matron snapped the neck of anything
still struggling, and we ransacked the human
corpses popped from graves and concrete crypts,
rifled through the stinking rags
for rings and watches.
We dodged skin leathered
like raccoon hands, yellow bones,
teeth with eyes.

EPISTLE FROM A SUNKEN CITY

You could say it was my curse
to be the one-eyed tender

of sacrifice, fingering bones
in a rural reliquary,

or you could say
it was my single mercy.

I counted teeth, stalked
the half-eaten coast,

the marsh heaved its heavy
green. I knew a little

of the bluing world
past the storm funnels,

when he came from the other shore
of time to string the powerlines,

reduced my sky's chaos to one humming
string. Sometimes he fished

the narrows, rowed home, then kneeled
in my dirt-floored temple.

We traded my magic eye
between us, and the thickening

breaths, the truthtelling. No
ship's figurehead, never anyone's

argument for living,
I didn't know promises

could die.
I couldn't see the cost

of his designs. To build a city
out of swamp,

to suspend it over tides:
its deep-down,

cruel stakes
bit through the pacts we'd made.

He tuned the future
backward as he left

the ringing water
to reclaim me,

gull cries unraveling
our history.

I sleep submerged,
my pillars greened,

powerlines slinking
in the undertow.

THE PART-TIME PENITENT'S GUIDE
TO MODERN FARMING

We own what belongs to us whether we claim it or not.
Sarah M. Broom

I am not back then,
I'm not a fallen monument, hole-bitten flag,
bayou village afire. But I was
born on a farmland acre,

dogleg off the two-lane
to Highway 44,
a farmland acre—its grass
just like the grass across the road.

I am not back then, when we took
horse teams and backhoes,
flattened burial mounds,
took rakes and dragged our disregard
across the earth.

We ravaged any pasture
like locusts, stripping every thistle,
eating every stiff or wiggling grub
that we dug up and said,

It's just some soulless thing
I found in a woods,
not even something's parent,
and I'm hungry and can't help it.

I can ignore what is not me.
I am not the past,
but I was born a mile from it,
where blackberry thorns
run along the fence

behind the honky-tonk
to the courthouse, memory
of pistol smoke and hoofbeats,
shouts of the disappeared.

I may not be the past,
but I was born right on top of it.
I grew right in it,

hoed out furrows, stuck my fingers
in the soil, made cradles
for the baby kernels
that would sprout new corn. It came up white—

Silver Queen, Ambrosia, Country Gentleman.
Doesn't everybody have to make a living?
Doesn't everybody have to leave
their own heart in aspic sometimes,

close up the jar, heartjelly,
ditto your old folks
and all their unspeakable deeds.

Please, I'm trying to ignore what is not me,
so can we also jelly
our every guilty gene
and stick them in the fridge
where they will keep?

My old folks had a slop jar like that
way back. They stowed it in a sea chest
clear across the Atlantic,

dumped it in some fields they found here
that looked empty, said,
These are just one or two lonely fields.
They would be better planted

with chunks of our hubris.
And then they grew.
Ugly brown buds clumped up high
on the stalk, unfurled their spiky wings,

spilled fluffy white guts over
field upon field of pitiless
rows. Upland cultivars, white
varieties, Coker, Deltapine. History

bleeds us all for its tax, some for more,
digging down into every wet wound,
digging down among the taproots, under old folks'
marble tombs or unmarked graves,

mass graves—there is no ceremony
under cotton fields,
just old folks, wronged.

And I am standing on that soil,
trying not to hear them.
I feel bad about it all, but

I'm just trying to listen to my headphones,
I'm just trying to weed these pole beans,
I am just on my lunchbreak,
I'm just trying to get by, and besides,
who can afford
to pay a debt that's figured in lifetimes?

Some nights I hear voices
beneath the oil refinery's hum,
and Sundays when it's quiet
I hear them, hymns
of all the faded parishioners.

What they want
is to come home, come home,
to have their faces recognized.

Tonight, their chorus
drowns out the cicadas,
it swells and swells
until it almost eats me.

OK! I say, *Well, then I* am *the past.*
But I'm still standing idle, empty-handed,
neck deep in well wishing.

IV

BARATARIA BAY, LOUISIANA

1

I know the leagues of it,
its compass,

the way the air tastes
of fishrot and humus.

I know its cane brakes and milkweed,
knots of wood duck and grackle
dotting the cattail marsh.

But even as a kid I'd trace
the map lines, routes
that one day drew me
upriver, all the way

to its northernmost source,
to limestone bluffs
that course with glacial runoff.

To return to the city,
at least one of the mind,

the weather-beaten town,
the bay of the mind,
its toxic islands.

To return to the rim
of a childhood
landscape—a coastline

even as it blurs,
disappears in cubic feet—
is to expose your own
composition, reveal your basic dirt.

I want to go back,
to stay what escapes
its own outline,

grab a few handfuls
of silt.

2

Say my past is a site
of battles and pirate coves,
of shrimp camps, black mangrove,
gas wells and airboats.

Say I do go back,
but not in person,
to survey what I have abandoned.

I dig memory's sediments,
see through satellites,
through lore,
the tender web of grief.

I find the map of Grand Isle,
skim my finger along the screen,
trace its movable edges

up toward the bay,
a place that is not a place,
a plain solitude in debate

with disappearance, a maw
that eats itself,
impossible.

I click a photo,
cannot recognize featureless
ripples pooling black with oil—

then panic, disoriented—
I have forgotten how to be at home
in moving water.

3

A delta is made by the water's will.
It gathers its silt, its quartz, its feldspar

mud, bears its fishbone and *sac au lait,*
gathers its heft, its trouble and storm.

The estuary, border without border,
tide of transition, freshwater to salt,

catfish skirt reeds in the shallows,
a gray whale's fluke scales the horizon.

A dredger appears, its black hull
barnacled, plows upriver, muddy water roils
in its wake,
                    then not a dredger,
a revenant galleon, fat-sailed,
it climbs the river's spine,
without humility.

And now I write myself back down
that river to claim a stake
in the place,
in the history

of winning and losing,
as if I could tally unsettled
debts, balance the book
of who took and who gave.

4

My mind makes turns
along the bends and folds of past

water, as if to track the shapes
of all the griefs
it carries,

the galleon, a war ship, a barque,
a Guineamen cargo ship, a tanker.

Escape calls the bullfrog,
Run away, the whippoorwill.

The water tingles with the memory
of those who could not flee
the cannon fire, the slow burn,
the anvil, the chains,

toward higher ground,
toward snakeroot, bull
thistle, slippery elm,
earth remedies.

Far away, upriver,
the cattle low, the smoke
blows back toward the Gulf
over the still
smoldering field.

Years have eaten away
at the myth that tall ships

ever delivered simple freedom
to this coast.

Years are eating away at the shore
where Spanish soldiers
first set their feet,

where the salt marsh is spooned dry,
its grasses browning,
mud jeweled with blue crab claws,

a lip of sand, its edges chemical-crusted,
sharp and sweet, the stink of crude in reeds.

5

The flat of my hand
on a tepid cup in a cruel

northeastern winter.
The webcam frames Lake Itasca,

a sweep of ice visible
beneath hives of swirling snow.

It weeps a stubborn ribbon
of still-flowing water.

I touch the screen. *Here*
is where it becomes
the Mississippi, gathering force
down the whole watershed

through the tributaries of empire
that fed the patchwork colony.

I believe that I can see
across centuries, laying claim to this or that
tidal bore, puddle of muck.

This distortion
is a kind of memory
working its prisms.

This regret—an indulgence,
but I see its hot breath

rise like mist from the bay,
the entry point
for the story of my own need

to trace the sea lanes
and dredge routes,
map them back to myself.

All these years
I have looked Gulfward
for forgiveness,

demanded that the dying marsh
confess what I owe.
But it's no measure of anyone's debts.

All it will tell me
is that I could never settle
into a cold, dirt hardpan

nor the silted bottom
of a riverbed,

but I'm still brackish,
coarse-grained,
made of tidal clay and sand.

V

LANDSCAPE, UNMOORED

I am tender of us in this American moment,
as we burn through the early century, our credit

suddenly as dicey as the waters, as this whole
deathship, breaking free from its rotten moorings.

I am tender of our flawed cargo,
of our air-conditioned doorways and neon

lawns, the way their alien green usurps desert and plain
impartially. I know our need, it is vast and flat-voiced

as a trumpet solo, needling us inside our alloyed
skins, needling its way out and snaking over our fat

borders. From the mast I can see the ocean
licking at that line we drew in the sand and dared

all comers to cross. I am already lonesome
for our swagger, its all-night wattage powering

the cityscape's virtual daylight. Our express buses
wobble their exhausts ever inward and circle

the cul-de-sacs of subcutaneous suburbs.
Down there in that heart, my heart

is a wistful football stadium stuffed
with packing peanuts to muffle those feelings

that might short-circuit the scoreboard.
I will miss the way we never mean to

unless we do, the way funereal ice tinkles
in our highballs as we launch

unreasoned assaults that spread their canopies of fear
across the known universe. Or say, the way

my own hand curves around an iced coffee's plastic
circumference, drips condensation,

my *personal* trickling into our *national* excess
that then pounds its waves into other sovereign

shores. So-called virtue, I can see you fade beyond that line
where the ocean disappears into the sky. You are like

a dream of me, neat doppelganger, or my better
self, who knows the right thing and always does it

anyway, unlike the real me with my regular molecules
feeding on sloth and fantasy, goading me and goading

me to push my most earnest deckhands onto the gangplank.
Our luck stays open all night in high season, but when the credit

runs out, it snaps itself shut with Tupperware
efficiency. I will even miss our failure.

Our comeuppance creeps like floodwaters,
swamping the decks. And from the depths they rise,

seeping up from steerage, grabbing for the helm, they
of the world's unsung legions, of the leastmost

bling. We tack toward the future, and bleak
is our aching turn into the wind, bleak is my waking

over the deck of the deathship,
lashed as I now am to its mast.

and almost bearing up
beneath the self-inflicted storm—

BAYOU MANCHAC LOVE REPORT

How many overboard lotharios does it take
to wrangle a disabled girl, hogtie her
to a fish story? Five knots past

the waterspout, and way more treacherous,
randy boatmen dredge for girl lips
to wrap around their briny

daydreams. Men moon about
in their pirogues, gorged on rumors
of sirens, as in bevies,

as in plural, who wiggle
fishtails, flash creamy underbellies,
through bayou gloom.

How does desire lay
its claim through thick water?
Men imagine barely legal spreads

of scuffed-up innocence
in forms made more perfect by longing,
fleshy like Florida manatees, but way more

bendy. Husbands return on the regular,
exhaust the shore with their hunger,
flashlights spark a pilgrim galaxy

in mist. One wades through his spell
hip-boot deep, dangling alligator bait,
calling, *Pretty please, mermaid, wiggle*

my way. What if it's a girl bred on benzene
punch, elixir of vinyl chloride, poured
free from the trailer faucet,

who now trawls that bayou, tough
as possum teeth? Sometimes
a sweetgum tree gets bitter, cries

its prickly seeds, and so does a girl
who's been hunted so long she almost forgets
she is human. What if one day

she answers the fisherman's
whimper: *OK, I'll show you
what I am.*

She breaks the surface, arcs a slender neck,
an arm that ends in flippered fingers.
They grab for the rim of his boot.

THE REVENANT ADDRESSES THE VICTIMS, 2005

A long time ago I stole away in a stolen
pickup with an old guitar, a mouthful
of dust, a ruthless two-step, and a single
flip flop. That was the only way out
of town except by prison bus,
fishing boat, or funeral
second line so slow
it could barely outrun
the past. You could say I have no
real business hereabouts, stranger
as I now am to your suffering.

And, yes, it's true I took
more sugarcane than I was due
and a bucket of baitshrimp, some truckstop
pancakes and lore. I hoarded street songs
I had no right to, and I aimed to win and made mash
from that sugarcane and bathtub rum
and never even let you take a sip.

        But, citizens, I'm back and flush
        with permits and chutzpah,
        bearing street cred, stock
        futures, and retro spectacles.
        Let's start this recovery
        as the last drops of rain
        spit down on the empty
        Riverwalk promenade.
        Let's crack open that final fifth
        and ice down our grudges.
        The generator's busted,
        and we're stuck here
        for the foreseeable
        with nary a sedative
        or corporate sponsor.

Back then I'd clamber over the leaky
riverpump into a basinful of Bourbon Street
runoff and drink my fill.
I'd swipe licks and lyrics from the loneliest
old bluesman left picking
at the cobwebbed corner of St. Claude
and Dumaine.

Back then, I lived on Airline Highway
where they still paid cash for gold.
I swapped lipsticks and lines
with bouncequeens and dragqueens
in the Bourbon Pub bathroom,
when the only way out of town
was down the drain.

But I have resurfaced
in the company of foreign artisans
who can make jewelry
from your drowned insects.
I have sketched out
a plan for recycling the city
on this paper bag,
the grid its revision,
to be realized
in bamboo and faded
Mardi Gras beads
like the ones that still sprout from balconies
down Royal. Step right up, my friends,
and welcome to your new
you. We'll hold hands
across the watery chasm
in the middle of your narrative
and marry your desperation
to the hard facts of fantasy
real estate.

Remember when the moon was so high
on dirty speed that it grimaced
and ground its teeth,
shot out the streetlights
on Magazine, and looted the antiques stores?

When gray morning souped
down the alleyway,
I picked through glass,
wondering what could ever
make me whole.

Remember when they shot up
that solid city block
of concrete, carving Armstrong Park
with bulletholes? I watched the bodycount climb
from the other side of Rampart.

I began to cross that park alone each night,
tried to trip myself into its deathtrap,
dared its swamp of despond
to suck me under, used it
as I'm doing now
for my own
shameless payoff.

Let's giggle
into our Sazeracs
at the new bistro on Dauphine.
You know, from cynical
engineering, we are erecting
our own kind of criminal
city, with a clean skyline where the jagged
people used to live. Look, there's a street busker
from the old days, a poor slovenly remainder
still sucking deathjuice from the margins
of the Marigny. They say he escaped
Parish Prison in the flood, but I know him
from my private geography. He has just
his one soil of origin that has sadly
washed into the Gulf.
His eyes spark with recognition
when he sees my face,
but I hear the developer in me tell him:

Take your broken shackles, dirty
blanket, take your clarinet.
Take your whole two hundred pounds
of regret, and shelter it under your lost
insurance money. Take a nothing
and multiply it by however many griefs,
and that's the sum of you.
This is how I say what I fear—
that there is no heart here
anymore, this is a place you can't fix
yourself, and there is not always a reason.

I slip him a twenty,
avoiding his eyes,
and this is how I say
I am sorry for it all,
but I don't know you anymore.
Rare winds tease the corner of my cocktail menu.
Huh. Must be a storm coming.

THE MARDI GRAS BALL, 1999

Governor, hold my bubblegum
while I ransack your dreams,
bruise my shins on your oyster-
         shell parking lot,
sweat my little girl sweat
between your knees.

You don't know me,
but I see your fantasy death maidens
in tubesocks, horny snow whites dipped in blood,
         electric milkmaids pulsing under their skins.

You don't know us.
We say *fuck* and are gigantic, straddle
         your sawn-off giggle stick,
then stomp around the train-set city,

         but soon we are alone
with our bigness and firecrackers,
eyeliner and moonbeams.

CHALMETTE, LOUISIANA, 1988

The night bleeds through its sequins,
drips black moss and sugared
pralines by the pound, in his Mustang fogged
    with sweat and Jungle Juice,
then in the yard. She loses her high heels
and plastic daiquiri cup,

trips past the yellow driveway dog,
the mason jars and shards
of old pottery, the backyard porch swing
    looping out of sight.
And somebody's speakers hiss with
Whitesnake, Whitesnake.

Riverbank grass is damp on her back.
Here I go again in the still of the night.
Refinery lights, toxic ghosts, love
chugs upstream at half mast
    like the barge,
stowing its melancholy and coal.

HOW A PROFITEER CUTS LOSSES, 2010

I took a skinny finger of coast,
dredged it, flayed it wide open, let it soak
under saltwater till it shriveled up.
I laid a capillary and pustule
system of pipe, drilled offshore till that
gray and white vista bloomed derricks. Hunted
up roughneck yokels with names like Baptiste,
Butterbean, and figured their use. I tied
their futures to platforms, for ballast.
When the siren sounds—no, fails—my masterwork,
my scaffold of promises, ruptures into flame.
It hemorrhages massive black loss, but I can
still cut bait, steer my speedboat by methane-
fire light, cut through blood-thick waves,

and underneath them, all the little dolphins
        with their blowholes,
                            gasping.

AT CONGO SQUARE, 2015
remembering the Illustration by E. W. Kemble

I strolled past the live oaks,
the historical marker—then stopped,

turned back, my face prickling
with a sense of the uncanny—

this too-familiar image
on a plaque I'd never noticed.

Somewhere a streetcar dinged,
my seeing seemed to double up,

the instant to shift, some bells and bamboula
drum to seep from air or memory or maybe

from the apartment window up above,
its green shutters thrown open.

The drawing is of the square itself
in the early days of New Orleans,

its spangled glory and shame:
a ring of singers and musicians

out of a Sunday and sketched—
I could now see—in bloodless

simplicity, the features uniform
from face to face, each mouth

open to the same round note.
It is a violence of depiction

that one dancer seems to recognize.
A man in the center, posed in invitation,

extends his arm to draw in a woman,
her foot turned delicately toward him,

and she poised to seize a rare and ringing
instant of freedom, meets his hand,

but is hesitant, resisting
with her shoulders,

as if she sees
that even in this act of release

she will be captured
by the eyes that bind her

on all sides.
And I felt the full weight of my body

in my feet, a tingling
between me and the paving stones,

as the artwork's full offense
fell on me for the first time,

and I saw plain my own failure
to witness.

And do I do this woman further violence
now, in this description?

I feel the fences of the square
draw me back

to stand beneath the live oaks,
watching, unwilling

companion of Kemble himself,
who seems to breathe beside me

as I wonder if any art can atone,
atone, the very word is like a bell.

DANZIGER BRIDGE, REDUX

Police gunned down 17-year-old James Brissette and 40-year-old Ronald Madison, who were both unarmed, and wounded four others on Sept. 4, 2005, less than a week after the storm devastated New Orleans.

"Five Ex-Cops Sentenced in Katrina Killings Case,"
U.S. News and World Report

The center of the movable bridge ascends
with a groan, the yawn of some bored sea god
now coasting past my windshield, the tanker's prow,

curved like proud shoulders, grazes the fog.
Plush white billows backfill
its empty wake.

There are two sides to a bridge,
but the other side flashes
and fades like an illusion.

Are there two sides?
Perspective spins
within the wall of cloud.

On one side, Bayou Sauvage, a wagon procession
snakes riverward, wheels and feet creep,
butoh-like through mud

as if a sub-sea-level pit of slack
has held the settlers all this time,
bound by the swamp's maternal reek,
their progress suspended in cricket voices.

On one side the river still lies coiled, vengeance
sitting hard in its gut, the Gulf still churns
its glass innocence.

On another the angel of history watches the wreckage rise—
boats pile atop the shore, cars pooling
in the elbows of offramps, whole houses,
ancient oaks uprooted.

He tries to close his wings;
the helicopter blades
beat him back, beat him back.

On one side an 18th-century manifest,
torn and tossed into the sea,
slips through the memory nets.

I have to admit the failing
of my onetime faith in structures,

child of America, that I believed
they were built to hold everybody the same.

On one side thirst, a pocketful of change.
A shopping cart wobbles up the onramp.
And on the other a Gentilly-bound cruiser
coasts, silent, lights whipping
the currents of afternoon breeze.

Then the gunshots.
And then there are no more sides.

A hole blows through the fog,
and the center of the bridge of memory
collapses, each of us idling

on their opposite shore,
staring into one another's headlights
over the waters,
their slow ache
through the Industrial Canal.

The bridge plate descends again,
clanks into place,
but answers nothing.

I put the car in gear, head for Orleans East.
In the rearview I catch glimpses
of the girders and abutments,

but the reflection drifts
like spirits and old windows.

I am driving over air,
barely skimming the metal grate,
like the bridge was never there.

THE SWAMP HAG'S VIGIL

I could say my mouth is a nest
of glowflies, of phosphine bubbles.

I could say I spit the greeny orbs
into the swamp,

and where those gases burn,
their ghost lights swarm skyward

toward the high-rises,
to stopper the throat of a tyrant,

burn the smirk from a CEO.
But that's a pretty way

to claim I own enough magic
to spark an act with a word.

I could say I used to be a particle
of cinder dust, a mite

of irritation in the world's eye,
one that grew, a kind of meat

and bony thing, a lump
that sprouted into human form,

and boom! I stood on the shore
holding out my two new hands.

And in them was the speech
meant for humans.

I held it there, unready,
then released these words:

Maybe I'm not fit to live
on solid ground.

Then give me mudflat or slough,
give me another purpose,

let me be alarm!
A red bell on a channel buoy.

But when the ship
blew in through the fog bank,

I stood there silent, lost
the faith it takes to ring.

I just watched the shipwreck,
listened to the screams.

I could do nothing then
but melt into the suburbs,

become another girl, potted
in the old South's nostalgic gardens,

the only way to *be* girl,
I thought, pink and dumb

as an azalea. I cut onions,
watched from the kitchen window

as the ozone spun blue circles up above,
a tanker drained its sludge into the river,

the governor tallied up his gambling debts
and indictments, his prison cells,

and I gained the wisdom
that comes from standing dead-

still in checkout lines.
I counted my hairs, grew hoary,

infertile as a mortarhole,
then stowed away in a flatbed truck,

slunk back to the swamp,
to settle my bones

between its deathless molecules of mud.
I guess I could be worse.

I never keyed a car, dug up
a garden, asked for mercy,

or smothered any thrashing animal.
But neither have I spared a soul

from harm. Instead, I let crude
fill my throat, stanching my flow

of courage. Now I want to feel
syllables squirm on my tongue,

to drop each word into the dirt
hope a fat green seed takes root.

I could say I'll call back
the silenced—the drowned,

the burdened to death,
but they won't return

to wade through the shallows,
leave footprints in the clay,

some trace of their living.
No gesture can summon,

no image can recover
what is lost.

But I keep a fire on the bank.
If a skiff drifts toward its flailing

arms of light,
I will open my mouth

and make a small
and human sound.

ACKNOWLEDGMENTS

My thanks to the editors of the following journals, where versions of several poems in this collection have appeared:

Adanna Literary Journal: "Jitterbug, 1953"
Narrative Magazine: "Affliction Parish," "Bayou Manchac Love Report," "Epistle from a Sunken City"
No, Dear: "The Mardi Gras Ball, 1999"
Podium: "Barataria Bay, Louisiana"
Slice Magazine: "Witness, the Levee"
Spoon River Review: "The Profiteers: The Chicago, St. Louis, and New Orleans Railroad, 1878," "South of the Narcissus"
storySouth: "The Revenant Quarrels with Weather"

My deepest gratitude to the many people who made this book possible:
Robert Carnevale, for his guidance and unfailing insight; Sophie Cabot Black, for her encouragement and her willingness to read and read this manuscript; Sean Nevin, for editorial suggestions that always opened up a poem; Erica Wright, for early and abiding support; Kristin Prevallet, for friendship and Trance Poetic hypnosis; Linda Hillringhouse, for perceptive edits (early and last-minute).
Albert Pulido, Amy Klein, Cat Doty, Mark Hillringhouse, Jaclyn Harte, and Red Washburn, for giving me a creative community that sustains me.
The generous teachers who have influenced these poems and my practice, especially Renee Ashley, Eric Baus, Tina Chang, Brandi George, Matthea Harvey, Tan Lin, Gregory Pardlo, Marie Ponsot, Patrick Rosal, Brian Teare, and Rachel Zucker.
Those friends and organizations who have provided support during the years it took to complete this manuscript: Ricardo Maldonado and the Unterberg Poetry Center at the 92nd Street Y; Donna Brodie and the Writers Room, NYC; the Fine Arts Work Center in Provincetown; Elise Donovan and the Union County College Humanities Division; the Union County College faculty; Robert Ready and the Caspersen School of Graduate Studies at Drew University; the Drew University MFA Program in Poetry and Poetry Translation; the School of Critical Studies at California Institute of the Arts; Dawn Potter, Rachael DeShano, Courtney Andree, and the entire team at the University of Massachusetts

Press; Ting Bao, Aileen Clark, Mariah Corrigan, Roberto Carlos Garcia, Jon Herder, Alexander Lee, Katharine Mastrantonio, Audacia Ray, Karen Zielony, my family, and especially Maurice Thomassen.

And, finally, Dara Wier and Arda Collins, for their belief in this manuscript.

NOTES

"Landscape with Accent" bases its opening on the opening of Seamus Heaney's "Bogland."

"South of the Narcissus" takes its title from Lucie Brock-Broido's poem "Toxic Gumbo."

"The Part-Time Penitent's Guide to Modern Farming" adapts a line from June Jordan's poem "On the Murder of Two Human Being Black Men, Denver A. Smith and Leonard Douglas Brown, at Southern University, Baton Rouge, Louisiana, November 16, 1972."

"Landscape, Unmoored" borrows language from Timothy Donnelly's poem "Diet Mountain Dew."

"How a Profiteer Cuts Losses, 2010" takes a phrase from the essay "When They Set the Sea on Fire" by Antonia Juhasz.

"Danziger Bridge, Redux" uses part of a line from Gregory Pardlo's poem "Written by Himself."

JUNIPER
JUNIPER PRIZE FOR POETRY

This volume is the forty-ninth recipient of the
Juniper Prize for Poetry, established in 1975 by
University of Massachusetts Press in collaboration with
the UMass Amherst MFA program for Poets and Writers.
The prize is named in honor of the poet Robert Francis
(1901–1987), who for many years lived in Fort Juniper,
a tiny home of his own construction, in Amherst.